D0864958

BOOKS BY ERIC BAUS

The To Sound (Wave Books, 2004)

Tuned Droves (Octopus Books, 2009)

Scared Text (Center for Literary Publishing, 2011)

THE TRANQUILIZED TONGUE

CITY LIGHTS SPOTLIGHT SERIES NO. 11

ERIC BAUS

THE
TRANQUILIZED
TONGUE

CITY LIGHTS

SAN FRANCISCO

CITY LIGHTS SPOTLIGHT
The City Lights Spotlight Series was founded in 2009,
and is edited by Garrett Caples.

Library of Congress Cataloging-in-Publication Data
Baus, Eric.
[Poems. Selections]
The tranquilized tongue / Eric Baus.
pages ; cm. — (City Lights spotlight series ; volume 11)
ISBN 978-0-87286-616-4
I. Title.
PS3602.A97A6 2014
811'.6—dc23
2014007079

Cover Image: Noah Saterstrom, *Camouflage* [detail]
Cover image copyright © Noah Saterstrom
noahsaterstom.com

All City Lights Books are distributed to the trade by
Consortium Book Sales and Distribution: www.cbsd.com

For small press poetry titles by this author and others,
visit Small Press Distribution: www.spdbooks.com

City Lights Books are published at the City Lights Bookstore,
261 Columbus Avenue, San Francisco, CA 94133
www.citylights.com

The ensemble has the intensity of a complex mechanism, as precise and unpredictable as a clock activated by the weight of a given mass of condensing vapor.

Francis Ponge, *Rain*

The hardly open eyes
    The hand on the other shore
        Pierre Reverdy, "The Same Number"

ACKNOWLEDGMENTS

The author wishes to thank Garrett Caples, Andrew Joron, George Kalamaras, Peter Gizzi, Rachel Blau DuPlessis, Bhanu Kapil, Nathaniel Mackey, Andrea Rexilius, Noah Eli Gordon, Dorothea Lasky, Seth Landman, Mathias Svalina, and Noah Saterstrom for encouragement, support, and inspiration.

Thanks also to the editors of the following journals for publishing portions of this work: *Black Warrior Review*, *Big Bridge*, *Colorado Review*, *Columbia Poetry Review*, *Diode*, *Dusie*, *Jubilat*, *Jupiter 88*, *Sentence*, and *Spittoon*.

CONTENTS

THE TRANQUILIZED TONGUE

THE ILLUMINATED EGG

The word moon assembled its intestines inside the king's saliva. The letters cried. The birth of each letter contained one hundred films. The merged nerves dropped to the ground. The arrows were injured by what the speech spread. The microphone was looking for an echo to explain. The picture of the burst tongue offended the crowd. The birth cloud reddened between rains. The city's moan drowned underneath the first growls. The voice atomized the line between the children's clinging hands.

THE PROFANE OCTAVE

The moan designed a frequency for soothing aching pumas. The bees blended their beliefs. The blurted heap boiled. The tiny mouth of a green bird created a long pause. The lost signal beaconed back.

THE ABANDONED SAIL

The mirage nursed its swells. The sky surrounded hawks. The baffled voiceover warped the scene. The sound scored itself in the sky the arrow came from. The cliffs bloomed Atlantic music.

THE MOSS VULTURE

The gloss the egg left inside the lantern entered the moth glands slowly. The bricks suspended above the trees. The blood of the panorama repaired the rain. The soot hooted. The hidden stars killed the clouds.

THE INJURED WINDOW

The wires inside sleep blurred between the feigned body that evades one during sleep and the precise moment sleep awakens.

THE POISONED VOICE

The vibration of the swan demented the snail. The scene of the pigeon crossed with the sickened sleeper's tarp. The city's doctors polished their revolvers. The owl entered a setting that charged the walls with stillness. The room held the cloud in its amplified lungs. The sky told the sheets to snow. The beaks froze.

THE SCARLET PHONEME

The octet possessed an abscessed prowess. The octopus incubated inside a hearse. The octet hovered above a horse. The octopus of inverse absence distended. The oxygen unwound. The octopus inched into an hourglass and unfurled. The octaves pitched.

THE RECESSIVE SEA

The accident exposed a tiny song when the floating wires grounded. The protozoan organ played an undetected tone. The tranquilized tongue woke up in a cell. The trees blurred into a seed.

THE EGG'S ALIAS

The embers cloaked the sleeping storm. The photograph of a bomb placed inside a rattled out lightbulb replaced the wind. The bird-child's bed was hidden in the chimney. The indivisible sisters collapsed. The mirror forgot what an hourglass was. The pharmacy filled with sand.

THE CADAVER MOTH

The clinging wings.
The tiny skull.
The embedded boy.

THE FERAL FILM

The tidal nerves were moon-burnt at birth. The grass the doves grew inverted the canopy. The stunned deer fished for glass oxen. The ur-creature's escape elongated the animals. The statue stirred its ghost in a jar.

THE DISMANTLED DIORAMA

The antlers masked a destroyed owl. The snow unearthed the dead membrane's meridians. The mouth hummed with one hundred lips. The wounds arrived in cotton. The lambs let out hounds. The optical rivers became opaque. The hive replied with a silent creak. The clone replicated the patient's casket. The pelicans twinned. The horses ate cactus salt.

THE KING'S SILHOUETTE

The body requested the scent of fox corpse added to the host.

THE SÉANCE'S ELLIPSES

The false snow filled the grave with salt. The iodized sails lured the faint signal home. The illustrated ocean remained still. The clock strayed. The blood sank. The sodium sounded out the throat of the ghost.

THE ACOUSTIC PLUMAGE

The birds thought thinking dust. The crown stretched out. The redundant feathers woke up as antennae.

THE MOLTING MOUTH

The word glass.
The word hand.
The word milk.
The word mirror.

THE CORPOREAL CLIFF

The revolver's blast hoarded a handful of abdomen. The space opened onto the falls. The scenery's son implanted an ambush. The wounded boy became a corona.

THE ARROW'S CIRCUIT

The plumage evicted from the unacknowledged wings of snakes reset the dawn with an exoskeletal clock. The blind curves in the atmosphere rhetorically reproduced enough aquarium gas to develop an electrical storm. The moot voice of the paper vulture translated the edges of a closed star. The atrophied hands of horses crossed out the language of flight with a more careless music.

THE PLAGIARIZED REMAINS

The microphone embedded imploding glass in the mouth of the king's collapse. The microphone married a flock of shrouded grouses to the hydrogen behind an iris. The microphone unwound the wool in the chests of one hundred surly lions. The microphone trained the ants to pray to the birds colliding with windows. The microphone learned to swim inside an urn.

THE CREATURE'S ECLIPSE

The desiccated roots of invisible squids suspended the illusion of false animism. The immature minutes infused in a tree created the vestige of a wolf asleep in the pupa's husk. The seed's scared feelers etched spiders on its borders. The penned mane inflated.

THE CENTRIFUGAL SWARM

The lion collaged its exhaust with the frozen-tongued music of desert vines collecting water. The ur-rain flooded the forest with flames emitted from the soundtrack of a flag machine. The captive voices of branches split the waves in a pair of giraffes into the first eruptions of statue moss.

THE INVISIBLE VOWELS

The river distilled blue sky from the bowels of swans. The coral roses crystallized the mapmaker's chest. The ruptured harp annulled the endless ear.

THE STATUE'S SALIVA

The bees unblocked an impossible sentence. The puma blood hatched a hello. The blurred hands released roaches. The boiled tooth vapor eviscerated an eagle. The tomb hummed. The siren divided. The signal flowered. The fault lines exhumed a grammar of clapping.

THE ALLUVIAL TOMB

The translucent quail egg dissolved the word quail. The blue scales on the pigeon's tongue predicted the sea's circuitous prayers. The torn monologues injured the orange lining in the open casket of a sturgeon trapped at the bottom of a deep well.

THE PRISM'S NERVES

The phoneme's spiral skin.
The alchemist's driftwood.

THE ABSCESSED SKY

The mapmaker swallowed scattered iron filings. The magnetic breath infested a negative inside the cellophane scroll. The mirrors matched. The moon swelled. The starcharts talked in tandem.

THE SCRAMBLED HELIX

The constellations crossed. The names of all the animals reversed. The letters drifted. The seized wheat burned. The clenched word became an accomplished cliff.

THE DISSECTED BREATH

The alluvial flesh.
The bleeding wingprints.
The bowed heads.
The missing glyph.

THE CORRODED BLOOD

The house of buzzing children animated a cadaver. The concealed seams fused with the weather from another town. The king's congealed head assembled its stingers. The bed's brains retracted. The haunted spokes of the spires tuned in sparks.

THE WOUNDED MIRAGE

The city's sickness nested in the mouth of the fountain. The blind hands removed a negative spleen. The detonated desert reset the savanna. The bad vowels were bled. The hills contracted. The malady halo remained.

THE MICROPHONE'S MOAN

The frequency for speaking through feathers decoded the owls in the distance. The projector posed as the skin of a parchment devoted to datura leaves. The codex spliced a photo of hives with the names of newborn stars. The references bred. The curtains corroded. The foam pools painted over a locust.

THE DRONE'S ORBIT

The flock spotted the scalpel suspended behind the figure's back. The moths dubbed over the moon. The sisters spilled out. The vultures dissected the scarlet cathedral. The snow was bleached with sod.

THE PANORAMIC MURMUR

The museum of crystal instruments.
The museum of glossed voices.
The museum of half-heard variations.
The museum of paper suns.
The museum of escaped lightning.
The museum of anything blinking.

THE POSTHUMOUS GLASS

The window appeared between the ambulance and an ant's shadow.

THE MEMBRANE'S COLLAPSE

The sleeper orbited the topiary ocean. The glass arms swam into the branches of a swan. The outstretched stranger dissolved. The solution steeped. The cornered squid stormed the shore.

THE MARIONETTE'S CASKET

The crossed out clone minus the wooden organs minus the puma projection minus the splintered mirage minus the orphaned eyes.

THE RETRACTED HAWK

The fauna machines oxidized the bodies of beasts. The fur-covered eclipse blinded the sky with blisters. The blood hibernated in a passed out star. The peregrine's aluminum claws unclasped.

THE EAGLE'S DOUBLES

The camera allowed two small children to try on the flag's new fangs.

THE INCENDIARY STEAM

The feral entrails of fireworks powered the clouds. The river beneath the river milked dust from the ground. The city's saliva swarmed. The expelled breath knotted. The cocoon in the king's mouth cursed into dross.

THE MIRROR'S SPORES

The sun crushed inside a prism corresponded with the x-ray of a chandelier.

THE MIMETIC MOON

The eggshell's fissures entered the word ocean. The latent spikes of the tide became bulbous. The scared phonemes frayed. The molting ohms mated. The migratory mouth coalesced in a voice that loomed above the umbrellas.

THE FLICKER'S SKIN

The somnolent.
The transparent.
The corporeal.

THE EVISCERATED RIVER

The ashes on the banks reprised the pollen diffused in the city's soot. The blind spots inscribed in the organs of an iris ignited the bodies of bees. The stingers hovered. The blank space blinked. The speaker absorbed the view from inside the skull of a pulverized asp.

THE INVERTED URN

The parallel tenors trilled to atone for the séance's ellipses.

THE INFESTED ECHO

The sedated cells of an immolated beetle winnowed into a seed. The mouth of the shrunken shell incubated an irregularly shaped vowel. The husk begat a mute call. The stem sprawled. The immersed egg's remains burst into ferns.

THE PHONETIC PROJECTOR

The sound pushed through the mirror in the sparrow's eyes. The view opened vertically. The center of the statue murmured. The letters bled from the sleeping bird's chest. The tone formed an ant with incendiary skin. The name on the lips of the drone spit out pictures.

THE DEVOTED CLOUD

The wounded grass woke up as snow. The word ghost asked for bread. The dust nodded. The house combed the attic. The speaker closed in on a sister's lids.

THE ABDUCTED DICTIONARY

The tranquilized tongue renamed its aphasia.

THE SUSPENDED PULSE

The doubled brother appeared inside the corner of an enclosed eye. The fluid fastened to the sleeping boy's head. The troubled lid steamed open. The reflections compared exhaust. The others brushed. The abandoned rows of scales revived the fuses in the twin's brain. The remains of the destroyed address entered a perfect circuit. The posthumous moan replaced the alias another voice once answered.

THE VESTIGIAL SENTENCE

The phonology of boiling bees circulated flesh around the signal's spine. The thin tentacles surrounding a throat composed a tangled silhouette. The small intestine of an incinerated statue spawned a polished ghost egg. The surplus buzz plagiarized two tape heads fleeing the wind in the fist of an owl. The spiral music of a mimetic howl reproached the cathedral dome. The full spectrum of helix species bloomed. The scrambled blood of severed animals recorded the center of a vulture's breast.

THE AMPLIFIED TIDE

The recessive films synchronized with the water in the conductor's bones. The stunted scenes nested in baroque ocean vessels. The host bottled the scarlet phoneme in a submerged physician's chest. The acoustic net dispersed a long pause. The tattered surface of a purr survived the sigh.

THE ATROPHIED IRIS

The fisherman's prayers poisoned the armada's lenses.

THE AMBUSHED BOOK

The encyclopedia of unwilling arrows.
The encyclopedia of injured silhouettes.
The encyclopedia of appropriated nerves.

THE FLOODED SWAN

The ornamental fluids of the fluorescent kingsnake illuminated the vertigo of an unfolding flower.

THE DEMOLISHED FLOCK

The word moth followed the burning fleet home.

THE CROWN'S COCOON

The cross-section of a dead puma's twin mirrored the vines surrounding the palace. The split brain rendered a lizard in roses. The animal's implicit plumage wore wolves. The scarred ivy opened. The amphibian fell. The fur of the damaged mirage rained.

THE COBRA'S POLLEN

The profane flora infused the sonar suspended in a single drop of ibis saliva.

THE EXPOSED STORM

The film of a glass of milk flooding the building filled the torn apart piano filled the closed casket of a demolished photograph of the sea in the child's chest.

THE OCEAN'S INTESTINES

The unconscious bed began to float. The sheets filled with petrified echoes. The encyclopedia of feral sails deciphered the amplified tide. The city solarized. The lapsing ghost abandoned its borders.

THE DISGUISED GROWL

The accident awoke in the wounds of a mammal. The inside of a fox burned. The blurred hands released matching fangs. The alluvial organs of the hive grew silence. The eviscerated vapor coated the snow. The antlers ignited. The redundant singers spoke.

THE EXHUMED ANTENNA

The sisters of the suspended flood split. The most devoted puma learned to swim. The sacrificial microphone swallowed its trail.

THE SPLINTERED LISTENER

The dismantled ventriloquist vibrated the street with the abandoned breaths of baby snakes. The frayed force rephrased the body of a delirious musician. The little fingers fluttered. The receiver evolved. The scarlet phone rang into a salamander spine.

ABOUT THE AUTHOR

Eric Baus was born in Fort Wayne, Indiana in 1975. He is the author
of *The To Sound*, selected by Forrest Gander for the Verse Prize
(Wave Books, 2004), *Tuned Droves* (Octopus Books, 2009), and
Scared Text, selected by Cole Swensen for the Colorado Prize for
Poetry (Center for Literary Publishing, 2011). He is a graduate of
the MFA program for poets and writers at the University of Mas-
sachusetts at Amherst as well as the PhD program in Literature and
Creative Writing at the University of Denver. He lives in Denver,
Colorado, where he teaches writing and literature, works on digital
audio archives of poetry, and co-edits Marcel Chapbooks.

CITY LIGHTS SPOTLIGHT

1

Norma Cole, *Where Shadows Will:*
Selected Poems 1988-2008

2

Anselm Berrigan, *Free Cell*

3

Andrew Joron, *Trance Archive:*
New and Selected Poems

4

Cedar Sigo, *Stranger in Town*

5

Will Alexander, *Compression & Purity*

6

Micah Ballard, *Waifs and Strays*